To Greet Yourself Arriving

TO GREET YOURSELF ARRIVING

MICHAEL FRASER

TIGHTROPE BOOKS

2016

Tightrope Books
#207—2 College Street, Toronto, ON M5G 1K3
www.tightropebooks.com

Editors: Ruth Roach Pierson and Deanna Janovski

Cover Art: Kalkidan Assefa
Typography: Carleton Wilson
Author photo: Krystyna Wesolowska

We thank the Canada Council for the Arts and the Ontario Arts

Council for their support of our publishing program.

ONTARIO ARTS COUNCIL
CONSEIL DES ARTS DE L'ONTARIO
an Ontario government agency
un organisme du gouvernement de l'Ontario

Canada Council   Conseil des Arts
for the Arts   du Canada

Printed and bound in Canada

Library and Archives Canada Cataloguing in Publication

Fraser, Michael, 1969-, author
    To greet yourself arriving / Michael Fraser.

Poems.
ISBN 978-1-988040-04-2 (paperback)

    1. Blacks--Biography--Poetry. I. Title.

PS8561.R2978T6 2016   C811'.6   C2016-901290-5

For Jean King

CONTENTS

LAS CARAS LINDAS DE MI GENTE NEGRA

CARNIVAL LONG AGO

SAY IT LOUD!

FUTURE NOON

Let Us Now Praise Famous Folks (well, um, sort of)...

The title of American Walker Evans's book of photographs with James Agee's poetic text, *Let Us Now Praise Famous Men* (1941), was ironic: The pix were of dirt-poor, white-trash, redneck Southerners, gaunt survivors of the Great Depression and skeletal ghosts of the great Dust Bowl. Michael Fraser's project here is less ironic; he does want us to praise—and to recognize—Great Black Folks (i.e. "Achievers"), from Ali to Obama, Lincoln Alexander to Malcolm X, Maya Angelou to Oprah. There are, here and there, hints that the Black History Month-style dishing up of The World's Finest Negroes should be taken with a pinch of salt, if not a whole truckload of the stroke-inducing white stuff. In other words, there's ambivalence about this poetic, ink-wash Terra-Cotta Army of Doers, Dreamers, Overcomers, and Never-Giver-Uppers. Sho' nuff, we's needs heroes—"role models" (the twentieth-century psycho-babble for *nat'chal* nobility), and folks of African descent—"us oppressed"—needs 'em more than most. But our heroes arrive, if not with feet of clay, then with "issues," often psychological, often related to "race" (which needs quotation marks) or *racism* (which does not). So, Fraser omits from his lyrical portraiture the song-and-dance maestro (or minstrel) Michael Jackson, or the current convict (used-ta-be "star") O.J., or the once-upon-a-time-Brit Black radical Michael X (who was hanged in Trinidad, for murder, in 1975, thus becoming an inspiration for the Nobel-laureate, third-world scourge V.S. Naipaul). Such folks are righteously problematic.

Instead, Fraser's project looks back to US Harlem Renaissance and Black Arts agit-prop, to the Up-Ye-Mighty-Race anthems of the Garveyites and the Rastas and the Great-Black-(Wo)Men-of-History scribes, and to the lyrical people-portraits penned by Afro-Am bards Gwendolyn Brooks, Melvin B. Tolson (see his *Harlem Gallery: Book I, The Curator*), Robert Hayden, and most definitely, Michael S. Harper. Tellingly, none of these poets appear in this book (and another omission is honest-to-goodness "Bad Man" Amiri Baraka), but perhaps their roles as gilded foreshadowers, as dazzling haunts in the background, is enough. Or perhaps they are summoned—marginally—in Fraser's poem for Obama, itself a memory of Derek Walcott's poem ("Forty Acres") for the 44th US president.

But down with speculation. 'Bout time for criticism, eh? So be it.

The second poem in the collection stages a reading of Austin Clarke, not the Irish poet, but Austin Chesterfield Clarke, the Bajan-Canadian novelist, essayist, and poet. It's first-person, this-is-Austin-Clarke-reporting-live-from-Timmins, but it's got third-person insight. This cub reporter Clarke, in the bush-league Northern Ontario brush, can only afford to "report / the blood and send the colour away." Faced with the sterility of skull-faced "hush" and unblanching "hate," the pioneer black writer can only "crave ... a wave, / a poured drink, a beach, / anywhere water is flowing." Here is ambivalence already: The loneliness of the (racial) pioneer. He remains heroic, stoic, even though he's "no longer the only / brown-skinned one in newsrooms."

Black nationalism cut with Canuck patriotism sees Fraser include black hockey players and former Governor General *Michaëlle* Jean in his *de facto* pantheon. One of the endlessly memorable lyrics is for track and field athlete Harry Jerome, presented in third-person, who "Like a child ... craves fire-fly glitter / suspended beneath his neck." Fraser is expert, throughout this fine book, in performing the Aristotelian task of minting gorgeous metaphors.

But he's also adept—enviously, really—at finding the incisive image that calls (you) out your name. So, his blues singin' Howlin' Wolf confesses, "I could never half-ass / the stage.... / [Woman] Scratched glass clear cross / my eyes. Called me Satan.... / hell is a mama that never wanted you." Well, well, well. Gotta like that earthy inkling of the psychoses of underclass *amour*.... But Fraser don't let up, won't let up. He images the ways of dark *Excellence*. So dignified Paul Robeson steps onto the stage of the page, "his words / sublime and deep as if a dictionary / had bore him." True: His meaning skids way past the Klansmen auditors, so "they stared again and / again, waylaid by what couldn't be."

I'm ashamed to admit that, despite three visits to Brazil in the past decade, I'm ignorant still about most black Brazilian history, but Fraser is not, and he is a true Afro-cosmopolitan in authoring a poem for an icon like Pelé: "In a polyglot / world, there is only one true / language, and I'm its ambassador." *Clarity*, thy name is M.F. *Charity*, thy name is M.F.

I think this book is an event in Anglo-Canadian poetry, which is usually about (white) anti-heroes: Billy the Kid, Louis Riel, even serial rapist and teen-girl-murderer Paul Bernardo (see Lynn Crosbie's *Paul's Case*). Moreover, these other portraiture poems tend to be of disturbed—and/or disturbing—personalities. But Fraser gives us characters who, even if tortured by their experiences of "race" and/or *racism*, win through to a stardom that edges into heroism, not just (*justified*) narcissism. The "Panthers" were bad black brothers in black leather and black berets, but they also "fly-kicked / and cold-slapped cotton-hooded laws with upstart intensity." *Can I get an amen?* Fraser doesn't just show his subjects with scars and flaws, gold stars and halos, but almost always with a generous, cinematic light, eliminating any notion of *Squalor*.

Compared to Fraser's expressive and cerebral word-portraiture, Franky Scott's P.E. Trudeau is staid as Peggy Atwood's Susannah Moodie. We want, honestly, "a sun blast cleansing ignorance" and a shotgun blast eliminating namby-pamby *belles-lettristes*. This direction is what Fraser is pointing us toward. *The Birth of the Cool*, yes, to prepare *The Birth of the Look*.

George Elliott Clarke
Canadian Parliamentary Poet Laureate
E.J. Pratt Professor of Canadian Literature
University of Toronto

"The time will come
   when, with elation
   you will greet yourself arriving
   at your own door, in your own mirror
   and each will smile at the other's welcome"

—Derek Walcott, from "Love After Love"

The Winter's Life

DR. ANDERSON ABBOTT

Everywhere I go
the future follows me
with oiled feet.

I hear her young footsteps
dancing on Dowling Street,
as my house rises
faster than iced waves
battering Lake Ontario's pebbled shore.

I see her smile
in the medical diploma
tacked to my oak wood wall.
My signed freedom papers
have taken up lodging
under maple floorboards.

I know the slave poachers
won't look there.

My cup fills with tea.
I touch the future with my pen
and imagine her ship sailing
to early morning ports,
the sun like a held orange
behind her back.

AUSTIN CLARKE

Since hate never lingers
in its pure state, I shape
evenings in pen strokes,
burn lengthened mornings
and travel to summer's dynamic
end, where the book is bound.

My typewriter clicks through
all those hushed times up north.
Timmins is colder than you'd think.
In crippled countries, men dice
other men for less. I'll report
the blood and send the colour away.

What my eyes crave is
a poured drink, a wave, a beach,
anywhere water is flowing.

Seasons continue to deepen
and drop through steel-framed
windows. I'm no longer the only
brown-skinned one in newsrooms.
I'm always on the snap. Somewhere,
stories are writing themselves,
rank tales, ablutions after rape,
someone's voice cracking the day.

BROMLEY ARMSTRONG

In the afternoon's piping glare
we sit like a Rockwell painting
embossed in the window's
dusted pane. Service lags to a stall.
Our waiter's eyes scrape past us,
withdrawing our table from reality.

The owner calls me boy,
collapses my age flat into
the greased-heel coffle-tile floor.
Other patrons just laugh,
shake outland heads and
pretend this isn't happening.

Evening fades in on cue.
We're still here, waiting,
but our shadows have left.

COLOURED HOCKEY LEAGUE OF THE MARITIMES

The puck skates in on parted-snow ice.
It's the season's last game, an encore
to stomach winter's sliver, to shrug off
the townsfolk stares.

The moonlit night is advanced in years
and highlights frontline winds. Streaming
sky trails squall skeleton trees.

Blades carve the pond.
Their cursive glide freer than
the north-rushing blood pumping
through them. Their thoughts
stick check to the gathering
freckled crowds. If anyone has
anything to prove, it's them.

If they could slapshot past
history's chain-link fog
and derelict promises,
to where falling white curtains
the world, they would.

DELOS DAVIS

This is the tongue's birth.
Words upon words, each breath
is a Latin incantation, an homage
to Cicero and all that may be right
with the world. Each courtroom is
a garden of chairs, an amphitheatre
where gavels are louder than
society balls, lit brighter than stars,
the shut box of concrete answers.
From dilating irises to encroaching
cuffs, justice is always an arm's
length away. The law for my people
is a trap floor. No one said being
first would be easy. What I want
most is to walk outside these doors
without the craned-neck epidemic,
the eyewash stare on this robe,
that unnamed suspicion and
disbelief from everyone, including
the consumed souls I defend with
the largesse of history sitting like
a heckling judge in every front row.

ELIJAH McCOY

It has always been something
I've wanted to unseat, the clean-cut sound
of metal rearranging skin and bone, that
incessant glacial image, all memories
frozen at absolute zero.

What becomes of these young brown
boys, their crushed hands left in machines,
the start of the blood trail exiting the back
door, the dialect of pain releasing their
lives in screams.

I confronted this misalliance
with draft paper and pencil,
funnelled my mind's lightening
muse to signal a shift in history.
Leave pain to the doubting. They
saw how the oil trickled like
constant brooks feeding steel.
That, my friends, is progress.

GEORGE E. CARTER

I know my hands lowered
as a seasoned man's spirited voice
scaled court chamber windows
and my fresh-pressed legal mantle
wrapped over suits.
It was the one thing he had over me,
a ticket to walk where he pleased,
and use that word again.

Seeing a mother's washed cheeks
was always the worst memory.
Why they weren't given books
constantly tied my mind.
Newspaper headlines passed by
on Queen streetcars. We felt their
gripe through TV screens and mirrors.
They watched me with all hairstyles,
and turned ball caps. Many could not see
we were carboned together. I saw them
looking back at me as if I had a choice.
If they had to go, they went
with the ankle click of my ancestors.

GRANT FUHR

I was down with Gretzky
in our back-ice hockey town.
Coffey, Messier, Kurri, and me
with tanned skin in winter,
a raging pride of upstarts circling
round goal posts. Edmonton was
the wild zest of hockey rinks,
northern lights lettering across
ice blue skies.

I turned pucks away and speed-
mailed them up trembling sideboards.
Seconds later, my eyes flew,
catching the Great One. His stick
a magician's wand, mesmerizing
players before whistling fans.
The goal light and siren shouted
with full lungs. We are winning
again, and my net is a story
filled with shutouts.

HARRY JEROME

Like a child, he craves firefly glitter
suspended beneath his neck.

He wants coins, gold patina skin. To have
that metal taste drifting between teeth,

the heat of concentration like a magnifying
glass searing paper. His obsession

with an unwinding track rounded to infinity.
If moments are distances between places,

a clock pulsing through rain, snow,
and slow boredom, trying to place brakes

on time, to outdistance other men living
between lines. The ground is a spring his

ankle fears. He rips down the straightaway,
holding off gazelles cloaked in wind.

HERB CARNEGIE

Trunked in the front closet,
his skates are still alive
and quicken each autumn
when local rinks
fill with water colour.
They line up beside the
helmet and shin pads,
like an old tradition,
waiting for the door to open.

He listens to the stick-carrying
brood of names
as jerseys slide
across the coffee table,
so many players unleashed
by their youth,
the thought of all those
lost years tying him in chains.

He catches games
most Saturday nights,
his heart unlinked to any teams,
even the ones who
wanted to court him,
but stopped in his shadow's shade.

JAROME IGINLA

Alberta born, yet Africa curls
through your hair. You're not
afraid of the outside, even when
insults hurl themselves across
wind-filled rinks.

Blessed with a calling, your feet
respond in propelled swerves.
All eyes follow the puck pinned
to your curved stick blade.
Like Houdini it disappears in
blindsides and re-emerges
in siren light, a harvest
goalies pull from nets.

JOHN WARE

This house is an arc buoyed
by low swaddling hills and
my sweat-drenched free hands.

I don't want to speak of my time
layered in creek banks with nettle
stings in low brush, hounds in stride,
or the full-mouthed lash horn cry,
how the limber jim riled my bare back.

I grab the joggling board uprights
and pivot the rocking chair
towards Alberta wildflowers.
I wave to my wife and pumpkins
meandering near the plank pile,
the air-cured tobacco smoke
escapes in puffs from my oak pipe.

These past few wet hours
have seen a congress of clouds curve
thunderheads over this stead.
I see more marshalling along a
half-covered horizon, the bronzed
plain brushing the sunset's lap.

LINCOLN ALEXANDER

Osgoode Hall frames hours,
eating is something we do when
the mind stalls, sinks to our throats.
I push back all the blanched eyes
soft-footing my skin like insects.
My words belong here.
Each book is a chance, every grade
a body confidence climbs into.

Sweeping the factory floor,
I'm a man possessed by sheer will.
The crippled phone. The job search.
The shade of opportunity reduced to
a glass of milk. In history books and
dollar bills, I see our benefactor
soaring with my front name.

Duncan & Alexander rides the lintel
beneath the fanlight's radiating bars.
I'm a man of many firsts.
Laughing with Elizabeth's heir,
the ambassador peppers a quail,
silver forks chatter. The uncorked
wine is a dream from lean yesterday.
Almost interred, my Aurelian
autumn smiles its presence.

MARIE-JOSEPH ANGELIQUE

The flames are incomplete.
Imagine this place without a name,
like my parched familial branch
scorched over years of salt sea.
Imagine the hate ash collects
when it cools. When it drains
all the numbed air had to offer.
Those voices within the coals.
Don't think of aftermaths assembling,
try to wade each minute's crack.
Uphill's wrinkled melody crimples
on a plainsong. For a little while,
there is meaning. Something to
knit a sweater to. The mob will
arrive when their feet scrunch thrums.
The wind's announcement turns
into more places. The blaze is
unfinished. Watch it incoherent
and half-done. Think of it as a
theme shifting into itself,
a complex sentence in mid-stroke.

MARY ANN SHADD

Quakers told me fear's opposite
is action, so I moved through days
faster than death's shawl could track
me. Word sermons blossomed in my

head as eyes trotted down two-toned
pages. I wasn't ruled by skin shade or
breast milk when my newspaper grew
from dusted sweat. No one showed

me how to install the sun slant in
lightless rooms or dig deep to
unearth my legacy. Still, the years
move one way. Incumbent autumn
is down the street knocking on doors.

MATHIEU DA COSTA

I hear the tremors
in their unclothed voices,
see yellow tamarack explode
in their near child eyes, autumn's
quivering heat gathers sweat
on their tongues.

Look at these muscled
half-naked men with their
lists of lakes and animals. The
words flow like river falls, and
I repeat raccoon, skunk, and
wait for the teeth flash.

All these tamarind people
watching me like a flower's pistil
surrounded by bearded gods.
How the blueberry dye paints
streaks across their cheeks. The day
is half-folded and whispers ripples
on water; the bell has sounded
and the hourglass has turned.

MICHAËLLE JEAN

Mountain hinges cracked and
snapped earth in a fly's wing beat.
Screams percolated up dusted rock
and waved galvanized roofs.
Everything was veined in stone.

The living stood at the rubble's end,
listened to the wounded sear in the
Caribbean's unforgiving heat.
My birth country stumbled against its
history. Flat bodies peppered streets.
Survivors cursed the ground's blowtorch.

There was never enough of it—
time. We jumped planes and cranked
our world's cupboards while doctors
severed limbs freeing wounded scores.
It was always more than we could take,
but we continued for those slipperless
street girls, each one reflected in me.

NO. 2 CONSTRUCTION BATTALION

Hugging scalped trees,
we listen as war's
thunderous train of air
rakes its way through
the touch of fall's anthem.

All around the base camp,
there are empty spaces
without rooms or footprints,
even places we can't drink
or pick up card games.

We have views where
the sky does not fall down
in slumped afternoons
waiting for the front to call.

We chop maple and oak.
We fight this foreign battle dressed
as soldiers, knowing the real struggle
begins when we return home.

OSCAR PETERSON

It started as a difference of colour,
the off-keys like me, varnished with
tone, and the majority that each child
wanted to be. My fingers pounded piano
keys till hours tantrummed into days,
pausing briefly for the constant fridge
refuelling. I flew out of liberal Montreal,
garnering the night's Grammy as I
awed audiences, cemented my spellbinding
style in the mind's slick highlighter.
My tunes took to streets, rag-timing
and following jazz joints where radiomen
let me drink at the wrong fountain when
no one was watching. Even after
the award shows and concerts, even after
the live television appearances,
meeting the mayor and governor, having
their wives, sisters, and moms air-kiss me
on the cheek, even after all that, I left
them with loosened jaws, then hopped
in a cab with my one-drop brothers to find
roach hotels that would accept us.

P.K. SUBBAN

You skate easily
with nets and history
at your back.

Your life tilts on
blue hue drawn under ice,
two essential lines
marshalling the hour's play.

Whistles decide everything
when referees stop earth's
rotation, and brumal
winter turns water to stone.

You've rendered a covenant
protecting a red-armed crease,
every approaching puck
becomes an assassin,
your stick blade,
the iron payback.

PIT-HOUSE

I can't forgive you for waking
before me and removing
your warmth for morning's call.
I hear your trickle pattering
leaves. This is a new kind of intimacy.
Surviving another night does not
anchor my faith. It's as if no one knows
we're here. Yet beside us,
Halifax glows in oil lamps.
Remind me why we are loyalists, why we
are black. Tell me why we are.
This russet clay ground has churned
mud through my uncombed scalp.
We are days away from food or death.
How stomachs arm against our will. This is
what we get for being loyal to Britain.
Tell me we are more than dust. Tell me we are
free as air. Give me new words for seasons.
Shivering, I feel the weather turning wicked
in this forest filled with things we could have been.

ROSE FORTUNE

She said, I hate when—
and paused in mid-breath,
with the sea-fed air
drawing in from harbour square,
the sun burning through trees.

Pointed sails grew in the sky's frame.
The ground's cobbled palm carried
her down to the pier,
and the waiting tote bags.

She dropped the world off
at the Annapolis inn,
her loyalist hands
loading the wheelbarrow twice
before leading them inside
to eggshell walls,
the fresh coins warm
in her side satchel.

She returned like a wave
to where their voices
bent in wind.
The boys stood with
stone and slingshot,
which dropped when
she planted her first
step towards them.

UNDERGROUND

They came like caged birds,
railed out in bottoms
of sunken wood crates,
their nostrils pickled
in sour stench coats,
summer's humid claws
baked them weak
while crickets squeaked wings
under slow moving stars

even near the border,
they were always one cough
away from the familiar
clinking chain bracelet,
the scalding half-tone whip
boiling bumps onto their backs
like a firebrand fresh from
blue hot fire

and when they crossed over
into Ontario,
the photograph showed it all,
Africans knee deep
in a vomit of snow,
a halloween of lies
while they listened
to the frozen icicle notes
crash one by one
in the ice storm's wake,

the strangled crunch of boots
waiting for the full husk of winter
to burst open

and in spring
they didn't know what to expect
with the new crops and all,
and when they dreamed of cotton
their screams shucked the night air
of its clothes
and their hearts raced
alongside the cold curdling voices
running barefoot into morning.

The Train I Ride On

BILL WITHERS

Evening on the bus.
Your mind moves inland
viewing the coming concert,
like reading a book one
has already written.

Towns pass like years, and
you think of when your money
rolled down an assembly-line floor,
the lunchtime talk of what if.
You and everyone certain fame
was a door without locks.

Now you leave
the past asleep in its bed
in a world filled with dreams
that might have been.
She with the sun's name
fading slow in your chest,
and the present that
follows you everywhere.

GIL SCOTT-HERON

So you listen to him
juke-jive trucking out and bustin'
loose heat on *the klan*, blazing
the hinterland when it's *winter*
in America, shakes and bakes
his way through broke bottles till
the buck groove slides pure pulse
into rump-shakin' foxes.
You know he's the real backbeat,
bonafide badass soul brotha by
the way he calls you "cat,"
his voice low-swinging
the "What's going down?"
You try to keep up, but your voice
airs out, all you know is *power to*
the people, and even your
granny knows that one.
He gangster leans when the jive
turkey pigs drive by looking like
heavy Joneses who aren't down
with slick threads or the outta sight
players. You stand in the stone shade
of his blow out fro's frolar eclipse and
imagine being the right-on dynamite
brotherman you've always jonesed to be.
But on the flipside, you know you'll
have to keep on keepin' on
to make it since the man keeps putting
a brother down, and besides,

he's already told you,
the revolution will not be televised.

HOWLIN' WOLF

I can hear the train coming
filled with *smokestack lightning,*
gold-winged sparks polishing
this slate-black Mississippi night.
Mama left before I could spell
my name. I walked barefoot miles
under telephone lines. Followed them to
Papa's towering hug. A dead man stepped
out the graveyard and tuned my
first guitar with spirit ears. Give me
a standard blues progression in A
and I'll show you what misery is.
Even near death, I could never half-ass
the stage. Although I was a tree
of a man, she made me cry last time
I saw her. Scratched glass clear cross
my eyes. Called me Satan with my
rolling, hard-stone living. Most don't know,
hell is a mama that never wanted you.

JAMES BROWN

I'm on the train
with a rail-riding woman
whose sable hair is lustred like mine.
The boxcar floors
are iced against my head,
yes   it's true
my mother left
before I could lace shoes.

Jail is a no-landing zone,
a knot of fallen decisions,
and guys with hard names
who didn't flinch
doing their business
feet away from me.
Even when I washed my hands
ahead of the food tray,
I knew I was one of them.

The mind.
How we stand outside it,
old and unwanted.
How each night
we fall in our sleep.
How somewhere there is abysmal pain.
Something my voice
culls from the wind.

JIMI HENDRIX

This is not the rich
homecoming I expected.

I'm dying with my head
stuffed in a porcelain god.
Where is the white light,
the electric fields,
and maples bearing women?

I gave America all,
but England became my bride,
accepting my mangrove hair,
density of lighthouse talent,
and thick upper lip.
Yet, the back of double-deckers
makes me shudder.

To you, the living, I say
sacrifice yourself to moments,
place your hands on albums,
sift through red liner notes,
curl into speakers,
and hear me breathe again.

JOHN LEE HOOKER

John Lee Hooker cut
my teenage afternoons loose,
and I was travelling light,
sleeping beside boogie beats
in freight train pickups,
stomping my boom boom feet
to pure river rhythm,
downing my musical tonic
with milk, cream and alcohol,

and I became a man
when he belted
serves you right to suffer,
a pine-top forest bursting
through brown cheeks and skin.
When rain wailed through Tupelo
I snuggled beside the speaker
and waited for a humming blue sun
to wake the delta horizon.

LOUIS ARMSTRONG

Named Satchmo after his school-boy
satchel vanished, his voice reinvented
a nation tumbling on its knees,
conjuring steamships and poker buy-ins
up the delta mouth of Old Muddy and quadrilles
circling round dance floors. His cornet
shook middle earth's groove, invoking
ragtime hits down Bourbon Street's
bedlam latitudes. He emerged from
nothing's torn retina to blossom-stroke
May magnolias. His childhood
double-timed as the Jazz Age
walked in from the future,
no more wanna-shoe-shine
mister rattling his octave mouth.
No more newspaper ink dashing
the day's events across his skin.
No more waiting outside doors for
his mother, hoping she earned enough.

MILES DAVIS

The day I met Miles Davis,
he poured gold tunes
out box speakers
and sailed ahead
out over coffee table plains
and climbed the foothill couch.
Each note carried its own light.
His trumpet called from the walls
and the ceiling was
a swollen cloud.

I was flung into brass moods,
my fingers pulsed to
the walking bag's groove.
I became a yard bird
with blues for sale,
a young rebel soul
counting the air-blast hang time,
all the hazed rhythms
taking a new wave elevator
to warm sound shallows.

Transfixed, I grabbed
onto the aural sculpture.
Water refused to go
down the drain,
time spiralled *'Round Midnight*,
the air lit itself
and glowed like a June day.

It glossed Miles' Italian suit.
My eyes rode the album cover
with coolness coiling itself
into my bones.

NINA SIMONE

I gathered notes
and allowed myself to empty
on trebled pages, my sullen
timbre unique as a morning
blue jay brushing windows.

On tour, my temper was
never off season.
Sometimes sleep was a ladder
I couldn't climb. Being awake
all those hours pays nothing to
the body, feeds heady minds.

America is too busy with
its illness. Like Josephine,
I smiled in French and was
treated like a royal sketch.
Love feels different in
another language. So does
this hickory coat keeping
the blood in. On stage,
I'm the watered crocus.
I am the star that sears.

PAUL ROBESON

At first they didn't know
the voice was blooming mahogany,
non-ethereal sound, born from the hulls
of looting ships and skin-filled galleons.
The arrival of canon thunder rolling
far inland, foreshadowing shadows.

They screeched to a stop,
when they uncovered its source,
eyes scrounging what couldn't
possibly be. But he's all negro they
mouthed, a dust-bag race wanting
to jerry ahead. Then he spoke in
walking bass lines, his words
sublime and deep as if a dictionary
had bore him. The meaning flew
past them, and they stared again and
again, waylaid by what couldn't be.

SAM COOKE

When they hear the news about me,
night crouches inside radios.
Reporters cease talking, but anchors
make disbelief rise before sepia stills.
The news intensifies around metal towers
spinning off into dark-matter crowds
hunched in living rooms or hemmed in bars,
bowing to the glass stone's glare.

A hotel room wrapped with my
lover's past is no place to tear
life's seal or dive into earth, unloading
this suede voice into yesterday's hands.
My wallet has ambled away. My pants
are gone. The lobby fills with November,
and I can sense death breathing from a
window. I watch and listen, feeling the
bullet's shockwave. I hear autumn
carrying leaves to the front door.

WITHOUT ROYALTIES

How would you respond
if a sequined polyester king
hijacked your songs and hip-wiggled
to stardom on radio waves
you weren't allowed to surf?
If the British mod raid
of bowl-cut *yeah-yeah-yeah* pests
belted out Afro-tuned jives
on Ed Sullivan's status quo show.
If you come from a Harlem
speakeasy with the renaissance
calling through your mind,
only to hear a beatnik poet
achieve fame with the
negro streets at dawn.
How would you feel
watching the home-run king
jiggle round bases knowing
you could tag his fat ass out,
and the riptide of cash
from all those record contracts
flowing into other hands while
hearing The Diamonds croon
Little Darlin' or The Crew Cuts *Sh-Boom*
minus that low-down, pot-belly bass
and sing-for-your-life black soul.

Las Caras Lindas
De Mi Gente Negra

BENEDITA DA SILVA

Sometimes I think of living backwards,
sink beneath wet concrete before
I become the five-year-old girl
shouldering water up favela hills,
working till night draws in.
I still see my dead infant sons walk
Mangueira's streets covered in blood cloths,
then day arrives bearing two white crosses,
and I rise to greet its hour.

Race is the unspoken thing,
a blank rift bookending conversations,
a sharpened-nail scratch beneath the eye.
Other ministers want me to backseat it,
to know my place.
They say history won't forget me,
my election wins have framed future monuments.
The past can't be returned,
but when you have jet skin, you know.
Former state governor of Rio de Janeiro,
I've come too far pressing this road
to halt my tongue.
Colour is only what you think it is.

CARLINHOS BROWN

This surging breakout rhythm
is full on, like a rooster's crow
splashing water on sleep-filled faces,

like a billion dilated eyes watching
Michael Jackson's moonwalk dust
the Grammy stage, or Apollo's precise

lunar landing. The federal government
wants homeless youth to disappear
under night's hired death squads.

Somewhere, I know little black boys
aren't viewed as raw felons inhaling
glue bags or a country's hogwash rushed

down drains, a reality I derail with hand
signals, drumsticks, and spoken syncopated
patterns. Candeal Pequeno, where my infant

lungs first respired humid air, now has sewers
skirting like veins beneath concrete flesh and
finished houses sired from my green largesse.

CAROLINA MARIA DE JESUS

It would have been worse if you missed
your chance, if rings belted your fingers
sending the bravery back.

Imagine your children eclipsed in that
mindset, what would've happened to Joao,
his adolescence ripped in half.

Think of your notebook, the stories gone,
residing with another's favela experience,
all your unborn words reclining in air.

Your stone-broke lines eclipsed all Brazilian
works in book sales. Imagine if you had listened,
knew your place, and set your pen down.

CELIA CRUZ

The stage flambéed by your vocal spark.
The hooked audience in full groove.
The crazed congas glittering Africa.
The struck-wood clave nesting time's cleft.
The radiated hips swiveling like hoola hoops.
The bent pain, sutured swell, and fried-jamón
joy of being Afro-Cuban.
The horn's prow drawn in searing embers.
The two-toned background singers rippling notes.
The song's shrill tales. The enclosed deep words
and twisted cavernous idioms.
The unpinned refrain leafing through ears.
The ochre-amber beads glinting like goddess Ochun
as you weave pennons over the piano's
tiered melody. The pewter mic awaiting seeds
to flourish into sound.
The flagstone notes they become.
The concert ripening in the constant now.
The plumed papaya queen drawing rhythmic
palms across the ebbing stage. The ridged
falsettos forging their own platinum medallions.
The capered feet. The pivoting speakers.
The first step boom of the timbao.
The bass rumble. The bongo's beat-down bata.
The half-pint estrella who's smile lights the sun.

ISMAEL RIVERA (AKA MAELO)

In the recurring instant conga,
notes rush onto the night some
from behind and others leading
beats between words. There is
colour in his rhythm, a visceral
truth no philosophy can unravel.

Moonlit harmonies plume from
stacked speakers, background singers
drive home freestyle phrasing.
The boogaloo beat-down spawns
sonal flashes, a call-answer dance
frenzies the crowd. If he had more
time, he would have built nations
tuned to the clave, motorways
underpinned with horns,
pyramids of stacked bombas.

Maelo always made good
visiting the Nubian Christ in
Portobelo, Panama. A meeting
of deities soldered in concert.
Back in Puerto Rico, where Africans
speak Spanish and Jesus is rice
over beans, he greenlights the mic,
lyrics bouncing out to the blood-stone sea.

JOE ARROYO

From Cartagena to Bogotá, we are all burning.
It's the inflated years. The banished hand-up.
The drug piles stringing politicians like marionettes.
It's crushed poverty clinging to hillsides beneath
translated penthouses. It's our negro father selling
snow cones in disparaging streets. It's the forty
decades of being invisible. It's our hair made for
cooling. *Pelo mala*, they say. It's bodies crumbling
around plantations. It's dawn's lease. It's the
infinite sleep we fall into much earlier than others.
It's the priest who plants our minds with insanity.
It's the god shaking his blond locks from pointed
church spires. It's knowing Spanish is only a
language. It's the whites hogging telenovelas
and all precious airtime. It's my lyrical prowess
nutshelling our second-class experience.
It's the pawned-off cops. Africa's rhythmic
call conducting our hips. It's being outside
any inside. It's the lessons unlearned. The thievery.
The debauchery. The corrupt inside everyone.
The slaughter of our homeless, glue-hazed children
begging for shelter. It's my calling. The promise of
action. It's me seeking justice from night stages.
It's the course beginning of all easy endings.
It's my voice planting hope.

JORGE BEN JOR

These words are kites
that become leaves,
cruising the sky's teal sea.
Chords ripple outward
sent from the scow's
curved sides. My guitar
is the land my fingers drift
over when the tan-tan slows
its samba to bossa beats.
That's when I find myself
immersed in Brazil's musical
seraph hands, playing to
halls and cup-shaped stadiums
where my skin shade multiplies
and dances under one language,
the same tongue our ancestors
brought across salt water.

MESTRE BIMBA

The berimbau's mouth kittles the green air
around Bahia, loams the russet former-slave soil.
Because nothing comes without discipline,
I carve hours into practice.
Lengthened days. Calloused feet.
A Tropic-of-Capricorn breeze circles
inside the berimbau's calabash mouth.
This aged colonial coin between my fingers
and thumb, strums tire wire.
Women with lower centres of gravity bend
under straight-leg kicks.
The setting sun fills with red shadows.
February's humidity is a dog lick across the face.
To see how far we've come,
knowing the fruit still hangs out of reach.
To think, we saved this country from southern invasions.
Even now, Queen Isabella's *obrigada* roams my inner ear.
Yet, nothing we do swings doors open.
Children eyeball the game, eager to tag the circle.
The berimbau jests, toys with rhythms.
They ask if capoeira arose here or in Africa.
No, I say, like all of Brazil,
it was born in the middle of the sea.

PELÉ

I never allowed my feet to
drift the way others did,
even when my age occupied
the area of two splayed hands.
I placed flags and kicks in
the collective mind slavery erected.
I shattered racism's edge and
introduced Brasil to itself while
Garrincha and I were TV heroes,
two of eleven disciples conducting
sermons on pitches greener than our
flag, the future's symbol. It's spinning
globe shouts, "ordem e progresso,"
order and progress through all the months
of February. When this carnival nation
started bleaching itself into oblivion,
I ushered in acceptance of black players
and distilled laughing sambas through
the ball's movement. In a polyglot
world, there is only one true
language, and I'm its ambassador.

SANDRA DE SÁ

I want to silence the earthquake
mouths seething fire at my
passing skin, how they summon up
memories of volcanic-eyed
plantation masters. This country leaves us
off flickering screens. In the morena's
house, television is bottled blond.
Its digital arm holds us back,
creates us in its own headline crime
image. See my coloured eyes, it's your
birthmark, Brazil. Creole sticks to us
like sand to wet bodies. The rich curl that
mangroves my scalp is loosened in our
pebble-filled streets. My dark cinnamon
skin is a paint stroke reflected in
clapboard houses, football swerves,
feijoada, and samba's long-legged cadence.
All of us measured by its common beat.
Imagine this country steaming to equality,
the birth of that sun.

Carnival Long Ago

BLACK UHURU

You sang
as Satan's Army Band marched on,
mashing up stepladder dreams
in the world's poorest
downcast dumpyards,
where the Cold War
was crewcut real,
and strangled nations
rushed the martial gangplank.
Everyday, the owl-eyed news
announced another one: Biafra,
Angola, Mozambique, Zimbabwe.
The blue-black screams
knocked at closed
United Nations doorways
as bullets levelled brown bodies like trees,
and back in mad-gun Jamaica,
you made it look shoestring simple.
Each bass-infected record was
a call to peace and solidarity
as your lyrics fanned across
palm-green hills and your voice
fell smooth and steady, like dawn rain
cooling the cracked stone embers.

BOB MARLEY

I am Bob Marley
of the tapping one-foot skank, of
country pickneys climbing guava
trees, of the shoe-horned ghetto shanty,
cut-eye Trenchtown stares, the ragga-
muffin style-man erupting smoke
plumes from dried rolled leaves,
prides of side-branch jobless youth,
of rhyme-a-line smoothies salt-talking
women with sun-softened lyrics,
the heavy, hard, rock-stone life, of gunmen
quick-ending dancehall nights.
I am Bob Marley of walking,
arm-swinging dubbed baselines,
the mystical musical obeah man
who nice-ups the One Love Peace
Concert stage, where Michael Manley,
Edward Seaga, and I joined hands
beneath Jah's approving lightning
bolts, calming the whip-tail violence
girdling my verdant Jamaica. I am
Bob Marley of the *congo bongo I,*
a natty dread rootsman, locks formed
from coconut oil and emerald sea baths,
singing picked guitars, clicking people's
minds, heaving them back to Africa.
I eat my okra vegetarian ital stew
and worship the conquering lion of Judah,
Jah Rastafari!

DEREK WALCOTT

His island days call,
embodied in sun-washed school
houses, and end in ocean water.
Rapt over crisp paper,
he wants all that is fresh:
the litmus unfastened from lichens,
or his landscapes uploaded to canvas,
women of all shades whose
tongues love in honeyed Creole.

Apollo heightens morning's green
echo, his patois voice dangling
over breadfruit, which villagers will
roast at Anse Chapeau married
with white rum, salt pork, and dasheen.
Walcott's pen confirms Negro Odysseus
skimmed this Caribbean skippered in
slave ships skirred from raped Africa.
St. Lucia's west-coast waves, string the
mythological bow with steady tradewind time.
For the writer, voyages ended long ago.
Home is when his language rustles,
and the oil-down scent softly
sails through the back door.

FELA KUTI

You sang *water no get enemy*
not knowing your blood bubbled
with death's slick viper voice washed
far inland past bush-meat poachers,
the sitting world of coffee truck drivers,
and human pilot lights painting Nigerian
bedrooms red with night. The Tropic of

Capricorn jammed to your extended tracks,
joined you onstage in hip swings.
The percussive narrative waved through crowds
as rhythm surfed outstretched hands,
the bass shockwave tracing smiles on faces.
You were president of the jubilee fete,
unequalled master of a growing harem, but
not immune to a novel grim virus.

Your weight unravelled quickly.
The continent beached itself, hid behind
a drunk healer idle with superstition.
The herbs didn't work. Rituals froze solid.
Even you must have known Sani Abacha
wasn't behind your downhill physicals.
Before shadows, your voice unmoored its
lateen sail, quivered airwaves,
and the feverish flame folded.

JIMMY CLIFF

In 1973 Jimmy Cliff rode with
me and Mrs. Alexis
as we rounded Cherry Hill's
breadfruit-green forehead.

He eased out the car radio
and planted biblical lions
and atrium-filled whales
in my tender head,
the car plum-full with sound.

How I wanted the rhythm
to continue as we
approached Market Square
dropping down towards
fish-scaled scarlet roofs
and the country women
behind foldout tables
laden with fruit pyramids
and my original English.

When the car faded to a stop
in front of Maria's Beauty Salon,
Jimmy's voice drifted into day breeze,
the afro age sat crowded
in vans pretending to be buses,
everyone bathed in island time.

LORD KITCHENER

Tell Audrie I sorry if I make
she sugar backside island talk
for thirty plus years now.
I said I never leave my first love,
calypso, with she perfect melodic
structure, but the soca bass line draw
me in hard like strong rum and red
sorrel. It was like taking a sea bath
and you find yourself as a breadfruit
leaf afloat Maracas Bay, on top waves
spinning to shore with the universe's
rhythm clearing your water ears,
and you step away from the sea,
feeling like the first animal
to spoor solid earth, dripping words
drying your body. Then you mind
yourself whining to horns and steel pan.
Even now I feel music caressing
my coffin, and I want to play más.

MARCUS GARVEY

Your voice climbs nodding faces,
brings street crowds out from darkness.
Yet, their will to board eastbound
ships is moon distant and desert dry.
You let words germinate knowing
another bent year under whiplash eyes
and children even more ashamed of their
backlit skin, humid-curled hair,
will round all to action.

Then they'll fund the Black Star Line
with unbarred minds, retiring doubt's
hawkish wings. They'll be all-in,
leading its maiden crossing. The follow-
up will be black-owned businesses
flooding neighbourhoods, law and engineer
firms claiming skyscraper offices
in every grade-A country, hospitals will
sprout where abandoned burned-out
buildings provided urinals for crackheads,
and the blanched media will say, "Look at
them, they did it, they really did it."

MIDDLE PASSAGE

Each morning
the dead feed miles of sea,
bodies hard as ants sink beneath
the Atlantic's azure veil.
Flaming wings of whips
crouch in inner ears,
cries blend with the ship's
sway and fill cracks of light
like tamped tobacco.

Sapped families stick
to their own feces,
cedar planks stained
with cat-smell urine.
Endless languages tied to stakes,
their memories kneel
like beggars in night's tomb.
Dreams roam forests
where hunters' voices
bounce off trees
hauling wildmeat
to fill hungry maws,
then the lightning flash
awakens singed eyelids,
saltwater from the fish pail
cuts another dawn.

Heaved waves
marry east winds,

brimming rains level
the ocean like a grey veil,
still the great waterwheel turns,
recycling the ash of burnt days,
sending them off to pasture
where wide weeks
grow without obligations,
where sackcloth months
count and separate
the nameless dead
from the nameless living.

ROARING LION

Music hit me well before nanny carried
me out the orphanage. Night was dry

chaparral with the other boys' blank
stomachs squealing hunger and snoring.

Calypso called me with its jab jab
and jump jump forming coloured rivulets

in San Fernando streets. The papping pap
tamboo bamboo herded the chorus of running

beats into the steel pan madness and whistles
erupting all around. I channelled words

over the roaring percussive carousel,
marrying melodic hymns with high-croon

mandolins and Spanish guitars. Heard horns
blare in, sending crowds quivering,

and when you see everyone jam and doubling,
you must know, Lion is the king of calypso.

SPARROW

You spoon feed movement,
swinging the igneous island's
coral surf-break hips,
dropping crazed words deep in
the volcano's lust-flowered eye.
You pedal-foot the stage,
bringing lyrical shade
against February's meltdown heat.

In another cold war century,
your green voice sailed out
of Grenada's French-named ports
and landed in plate-flat Trinidad,
setting the carnival ground ablaze
with lime taffeta explosions
and sparkling worlds bouncing
coloured light off bronzed bodies,
grinding a moving horizon of floats
against the dappled night's madness.

You on stage like a bald lion
thundering punctuated putdowns,
levelling all calypso challengers.
Your voice is a *witch doctor's from a land afar*,
greeting j'ouvert morning's painted arrival
and leading the Dionysian throngs into sharp sun.

TOUSSAINT LOUVERTURE

Night lies frightened in hills
waiting for the shoeless voices
to fall green from trees.

Each man carries his own light.
The ox horn's leaden wail
darkens the punctured moon.

Hours move in four-four time,
the sound of feet rushing
past the governor's mansion.
In the courtyard,
a lonely French flag
sleeps by itself.

Rumour races round corners
and makes its home
in the ears of slaves,
news that someone saw
the future march into Port-au-Prince.

Say It Loud!

CONVICT LEASING

*"Neither slavery nor involuntary servitude, <u>except as a</u>
<u>punishment for crime</u> whereof the party shall have been duly
convicted, shall exist within the United States, or any place
subject to their jurisdiction."*
– 13th Amendment of U.S. Constitution

Americans pried words open, resettled the day's
leaning. Soon, walking on sidewalks became a felony,
if you were black. They unleashed fines for "boys"
smoking tobacco. Most were conjured and thrown
before judges during harvest time.
Alabama lawyers laughed outside courts.
Smith created the most infractions after downing beers
and swearing up the tavern. Ma's biscuits were still
warming morning's larboard air when they bagged darkies
passing by the market on a cloud-marred day.
A black man walking was clearly illegal on Tuesdays.

1865 to 1942, they spent lifetimes
running from glints of Gehenna's charcoal pitchfork,
fell under old Jim Crow's strumming rhythm.
The smouldering sun needled into brown bodies
clinked together, barefoot in fields. Wearing canvas
clothes, zebra-striped prisoners worked cotton shifts
to heal their "fines." Sickness and luck caught the weak,
silencing their breath. These chain gangs picked decades
in raw earth till the Japanese slit Pearl Harbor open.
Only then did Roosevelt peel back the furrows
and unhinge the yoke from its oxen.

FREDERICK DOUGLASS

Yesterday I found
the person I used to be,
hungry—prone
in scalded fields,
looking at white herds eating
the nailed-up sky.

It took leftover pan fat
and two wood matches
to flame that rat-eaten shirt.
I saw the shackles
skin into his bone.

Words carried me away
from him and multiplied
in my weathered hands,
they spilled over lecterns
and shouted for freedom.

I took his ashes
and snowed them over
huckleberry bushes.
I listened with children's ears
as his thin illiterate memory
covered hedge leaves
and left me nothing but silence.

GEORGE JUNIUS STINNEY, JR.

The ground is bleeding. Don't think of
him as a kid red-rovering through
holly fern. Don't think of him as
the innocence summer fills with sun.
Courtside, minutes evaporate into

a verdict, setting air ablaze.
Don't think of him as a child
innocence surrounds. School photos
guarding elderly walls.
Let the instant settle itself.
1944 is half-peeled and ripens
like fall's oil-painted leaves.

Hunger spaces his mind,
an admission divides suffocating
hours of interrogation.
The promised ice cream cone
is a torn lie opening steel doors.
Don't think him green
without agency, a fourteen-year-old
immured by partial men,
no bar member to sandbag his words.

Think of your hands, your
earth turning without offspring,
a family forced to hotfoot town.
Currents wiring teeth,
a child's eyes looking up,
alone.

GORDON PARKS

How difficult to predict
the foldout future
while you collect hard grain
spilled on fresh barn floors.
The horse smell
raked through a harness
and the narrow hay bales,
bricks stacked in annealing dust
moon-miles away from
Manhattan's flight towers.

How could you see
the blond polished letters shimmer
your name like a billboard
ironed on the director's chair,
while you muck stalls
and watch the mare's blink-eye
catching your shovel's gleam
beneath *the learning tree.*

You can't imagine
moving your hands in camera clicks
as winds sweep the pemmican plains.
A crumpled Kansas rolls
you in the clapboard house,
your cowboy hat and the lightning
steps ahead of the storm's drip line.

HARRIET TUBMAN

Harriet grabbed the night
with sharp-eyed suspense.
Freed slaves didn't understand the point,
going back into the devil's mouth,
risking days of dog bite and whip crack.
It was the insanity of their situation
that made them mark words, continuing
like new turtles escaping to sea.

She could have said more,
letting all know what she saw.
Visions of epileptic trains in
a three-mile-an-hour world.
A northern land, warmed by winter's
wool sweaters, seemed odd to her.
Abolitionists knew her real home was
always the journey, never the prize.

Nothing came of lethal threats
to the underground railroad,
even the reward money remained
untouched while she swept chicken yards
under daylight's windblown mane,
incognito, yet out in open sun.
Around her, midnight crouched
in tree shade singing,
Go down Moses, Moses go down.

JACK JOHNSON

You were elated. Another pale-faced
challenger lay dreaming on knitted canvas,

his boxing gloves too big to shine your shoes.
You airlifted the pride of ex-slaves.

Your burden hung between Jim Crow's
canine teeth and sharecropper blues.

You wanted all, even the other half
of town, the side you didn't understand.

They labelled you uppity even after
you belted the great white hope.

Fear is a language you refuse to learn.
In the gladiator's roped square,

you are crowned world champion.
The white wives were the final claw

in a world hemmed-in with roving
mental disorders. You never ignored

places you weren't allowed to go, even when
the good old boys were whisky tight,

fetching to beat negroes. Endless hunger,
you didn't know when to stop. At some

point you're no longer green and bouquets
of flowers arrive when you least expect.

JACKIE ROBINSON

I was rain-blind.
The white spheres invisible
till gravity laughed them down.
Slurs jumped from stands
and wolf-circled my plays.
The crowd's voice was the
background hum conk shells
brewed. Fifty thousand lungs
pressed my ears.

The dugout was a quarry,
change rooms—nails to chalkboard.
Every game was an away game,
even our own ball boys were
hot-sand hostile. Hotels lay
dangerously beyond colour's
warning track. Managers said
I could take it or leave it.
I took it and triple-played
beyond my place in society.

I furnished my people with a grand-
slam hi-five, the ninth-inning save.
I bore the load and walked, ignoring
how edged shanks ripped my back.
Many labelled me "porch monkey"
and "uncle Charlie," a slave kissing
massa's knees. To them I say,
certainly, there were talented others,
but, I will always be the first.

JAMES BALDWIN

Yes, he was there in tight blazers,
wading slim pants and cockroach killers
when Harlem still had tinsel voices
and bebop jazz streets heavy in
cerebral flow. He stayed mainly
in his clacking closet and let eyeliner
lids wink that urge puberty brought.
There in his one skin, living multiple
lives, but always a negro in redlining
America, the one he tried to engrave
across his shadowed face. He knew we
weren't citizens long before water
cannoned out firehoses and banks
were suddenly penniless, refusing
to offer loans. The freedom rides, bus boycotts,
how Birmingham church bombs silenced
four little girls. All that gifted advocacy
roiling under earth. Even today,
if he were to rise out his grave,
he'd go tell it on the mountain, watching
the fatherless articulate vacancy,
and those stricken by that ignored
sinful pandemic spitting black lives.
If Beale Street could talk...
Man, *if Beale Street could talk...*

JESSE OWENS

Before every race,
Hitler's tongue is revved
to full throttle.

Fingertips balanced on chalk,
all runners lean
towards future moments.

This is how the starter
holds history,
one click at a time.

The gun blast.
Our expanding multiverse
carrying his spry feet.

The finish line
a flattened hourglass,
a white ribbon brushing skin.

KING

You gained believers
with smouldering words
everywhere you stopped,
the podiums draped
themselves in history.
Sunlight always flooded in
and parted gathering clouds.
Your voice thundered
over stone mountains
and dragged twilight
across waving blond plains,
a silver stripe binding the nation
in a multi-coloured dream.

Even in the face
of eager steel guns,
the thick-bodied water
erupted from hose nozzles.
The white-hooded cross bearers,
stoop-shouldered and seething,
stiffened laws that shifted
and sat themselves in
the back of long hot buses.
Even in the rain of thrown eggs,
doves flew from your hands.

LANGSTON HUGHES

The words arrive carrying a heavy mirror,
making you gaze inward. In Harlem and Kansas,
things are not the same. Our brewed president is
treated like a southern boy. The tea marchers
pull down houses screaming they want
their country back.

Langston, your time is far away,
so far away, much further than Africa.
Even with your Cherokee skin you craved
our ancestral wellspring, with its troubled
blues edge. Flames climb the sky's static ladder.
The new songs take their place along summer's
heated flanks. Language is speeding up. The old
books are running out of breath. The young
rename streets in protest. This is what happens
when dreams are shackled, skirred across water,
and sold on poplar stumps.

MALCOLM X

I hear there's snow outside;
nature is alive,
colder than these walls.
Tomorrow I'll begin again,
shake all rising bands
of boredom sailing in.

I wash the days with thought,
take muffled clinks as signposts
from light spades beyond this cage.
I brew spirits from half-eaten apples,
watch time march
the cement floor in shadows.

Somewhere there's a trial mewling,
an applause of camera clicks,
ink stretched across pages,
someone's footsteps released
by a judge's gavel,
someone who is not me.

THE PANTHERS

Because Watts was burning I dashed
watch chains and grabbed dishracked
sinks filled with the back-cutting weight of
my enslaved ancestors and buried everything
into store windows, blasting my hand-tied
Jim Crow past, all the covered-mouth rapes my
mother's grandmothers endured and flipped
the lord's shotgun back because I knew he
couldn't exist, and let the safety click
speak up in public. Because Watts
was burning, I became Huey Newton &
Bobby Seale packing intellectual heat in
mist-filled Oakland dawns, thrusting the bay's
glacial by-laws back at pearl faces
perched on painted-lady porches,
their eyes coding me behind police masks.

I moved rocket-fast and turned history,
pounding the 60's when everything moved
in Ozzie & Harriet time. Because Watts
was burning, I climbed out of the weathered
underground launching the pyretic distaste
of our soldiers felled in Vietnam, Korea,
the gas-soaked trench lines that carved
up Europe, returning to see fountains coupled
with "whites only" outside theatres
or clinging bat-mad to hotel sides. I couldn't
choose bus seats, but they let me appoint
my tree and swung my brothers with

hemp twine, swivelled their charred remains
under dixie suns chasing night's
blackened knees. I was half-time in
boardrooms and law offices, doing
the janitor's ragtime jig soft-shoeing across
marble, venting song and seeing
toothless laughs, my children walking
coatless to winter schools minus books.

Because Watts was burning, I knotted history's
apron strings and linked up with Stokely
Carmichael and Angela Davis to seal the hot
spot beatdown on racism's fireside flush. We
blared our jive plot points on our half-erased rasping
story. How we remained horse-saddled
in summer's cottoned death fields,
our sweat-sliced skin interred and spliced
by colour's flashpoints. We fly-kicked
and cold-slapped cotton-hooded laws with
upstart intensity. Because Watts was burning,
and turning charred brick back into black carbon,
I rose to red-glare, wailing alarm clocks,
clipped the magnum to my side, and finally,
finally, decided to WAKE THE HELL UP!

PLANTATION

For the long opened day,
we stand half-naked
in molten sun,
remembering we are dust.

The gathering weeks wrap
sharp arms round skeletal feet.
Sweet cane juice sinks
into ash skin
drawing ants to the feast.

We empty bowels like dogs
squatting over sleepless earth,
afternoon's whip-lashing glass
eye watching from all directions.

The brick-red sunset brings
the sound of startled triangles
in its darkening hands.

We dip bread in pig slop
and wipe the stench from
parched mouths.

We lie on bare earth
praying death's cloak
shanks us in night's tide.

ROSA PARKS

The day was sewn
in the redness of your skin
and broke into four pieces.

A thought remembered itself
and sat in the opened window's breeze.
All those hours in standing heat
while the bus remained front-empty.

Minutes stretched themselves
into tides of shocked faces.
Centuries shifted through watches
as police sirens held the captive air.

You didn't know your place.
Yet, you stepped off the bus
dressed in handuffs,
your feet swollen with the
sting of four centuries,
and walked dignified
into history.

RUBY BRIDGES

You and Ms. Henry create language
in a vast sistered room,
ceaseless as your imagination.
The voices you create,
talk to you from empty seats.

Outside, marshals slide crowds back,
their letters fumbled into words
Mama told you not to say.
The spit. Old eggs. Misspelled signs.
Venom bleeding behind eyes,
and you edging four feet tall,
threading heated gauntlets.

Your street circles in disbelief.
Neighbours ask why your parents
placed you in eagle claws.
Your father is now jobless.
The NAACP shields our hamitic skin
against the blow torch, legal shakedowns,
but, where are their children?

You don't know where the other
children have gone. You with a bow
in changing air. Hard to believe,
in one year, they'll sit around you,
petals honouring the flowers core.

THE LYNCHED

The veins of these trees
know the night's flavour
as it climbs and
washes each leaf
in summer's moon shade.

The aging bark listens
and peers through time
back to laughing crowds
with their army of words.

How the boy swung
over the loose voices.
How flies chewed his face.

Morning brings its scavenger tide,
an establishment of worms and beetles
crawl from the dangling tongue,
sound of something feasting
from the inside out.

How a man suffocates in air.
How a man breaks down
in the deadfall earth.

TRAIN PORTER

When I stay here,
the months have moved
and are now setting
on yesterday's sea.

Everything is the same.

While I'm away,
my children become trees
and branch without me,
my wife recedes deeper
into a brooding silence.

My smile polishes
the cold silverware
snarling back at me.
Break times we assemble
the white clay planets,
eating leftovers right off the clay.

Balancing metal trays
I'm always on time
when the steel coffins lurch
out of stations crippled with smoke.

Their pale faces come and go
as I shift down carpeted aisles.

Future Noon

ADOPTION

At the animal shelter,
black cats and dogs lift to smiles,
their whimpering eyes pursue
children through stacked cages,
offering what only unbridled love
can bring. Half price, or free, only
the charcoal-shaded are left behind.

This sable hue sidelines children
awaiting adoption. Even the
honey-coloured know there's an
asterisk beside their names.
The state is their den mother
till they "age-out" stumbling
into a mature ripened world.

The giveaway continues at
the animal shelter,
but few want to cuddle
the barking night.

AUTHENTICITY

Black is, black ain't.
Black is jackolantern-toned basketballs
bouncing bold on cracked city stone,
the currency of baseball caps turned
sideways, engaged to endless brand names,
the phat, mealy mouthed all-night
brotha palming neon-thonged booty on B.E.T.
Black ain't the halcyon calm of libraries
or skyscrapers of advanced vocabulary,
armies of young people in academic physics.
Black is down and out, minor chords
lacking responsibility, it's disrespectful,
combative and unresponsive. Black ain't
going to med school, proudly mouthing
canuck accents or playing defense for
the Montreal Canadians. Black doesn't
dish logic like scholars in after-school
debate clubs or attend the latest
documentary film series. Black is always
chilling in videos, pumping modern day
minstrel shows colonizing minds like
the word "cool." Black is outside the
inside, onside the downside, putting
the layaway on the freeway, criminally
minded and is always late. Black doesn't
read, understand organic chemistry,
play chess, raise its hand in math class
or write anything as endearing as poetry.

BELL HOOKS

I'm always about the other,
the drip pan drop of lost
opportunity reverberating through
stacked centuries, amassed neglect,
of newsflash highlight reels,
the baton bat-blow and
fist-pummelled brothers and sisters.
I harvest society in bundles,
harness cultural patterns into
books, show society its
mirrored face, harness and grill
the establishment's scrolls.
I make my exceptions known
on world campuses. My tongue
is sugar apple and bitter tamarind.
My voice centres lecterns and is
a sun blast cleansing ignorance.

THE CENTRAL PARK FIVE

If they could turbo minutes back,
they'd juvenile night on 112 Street,
teen kicks breezing local strides,
then check into their witch-hour cribs,
lives anonymous as brownstone windows.

But prosecutors must unclench careers
and line up for the election showtime
carroting ahead on the horizon,
before paper escapes to other candidates'
pockets. Detectives follow plain breadcrumb
paths, their daydream minds stumbling on
price-point promotions. Newsroom hype
renews the anchor's Jag and brushed-sand
steps hedging burnished Hamptons villas.

This is why they vacantly thin out
behind Juvie bars smelling freedom's
counterpoint as each day clinks
down hallways. They are new Scottsboro
boys filling America's racial debt book.

FRED HAMPTON

There are reasons for everything.

Reasons why Black Panthers leader
Fred Hampton slips through life's grey veil
in firestorms of midnight bullets.

Reasons why the FBI denies
all eyewitness accounts
to push their version of events.

Another reverend calls for quick justice,
warns against violent reprisals.

Outside's dead summer heat makes
white Chicago tip toe into
Lake Michigan's calm.

Within the infernal church,
choirs chant old spirituals
in a land we dream of,
a time we can't leave,
and dry hollow spaces we can't inhabit

one by one children scream,
"I am Fred Hampton."
"I am Fred Hampton."
"I am Fred Hampton."

JEAN-MICHEL BASQUIAT

Colours falsetto across canvas,
images unlock keys to interred masters.
Van Gogh peeked over your shoulder
and everyone called you Samo in
your graffiti-walled, coffee-fueled,
warm welcome Greenwich Village.

When times swung low, you busted
out the hand-to-mouth lunch squat-
down chilling in Washington Square.
Annina Nosei vibed your frequency
and sable-night Mohawk over paint-
splattered smocks, latching onto your
bonafide main street energy,
the cut-up, paste-up, be-bop African
jazz aesthetic. It was all boom-for-real
at the PS1 new wave show where you
stood on the periphery of an epicenter
world others created.

Fab 5 Freddy knew the platinum art
gentry would never accept you,
even with Warhol snuggling your hand.
The 27 club took you into veiled shelter.
Hendrix, Morrison, Joplin, Jones, Cobain,
and Winehouse doing the get-together
tango with you flowing awe.
Everyone wants to be part of something.
Heroin fuels the cross-over daily. If you

only knew, it's the other side of the painting that really matters.

JOE FRAZIER

You would have
loved to drop Ali,
like death-fresh roadkill,
silence his tongue in uppercuts.

With microphones
blossoming before your face,
you insisted on calling Clay
by his earthen name,
and the largesse of insults continued:
gorilla-ugly Uncle Tom,
meat-packing plant brawler ,
and the others you mind-blocked
out of existence.

Even when the lights faded,
and reporters watched fights
in the depths of living rooms,
Ali's words kept coming towards you.
Newspapers attacked you.
Odds makers froze you out,
even your own people
turned coats and walked on.

All cameras and tape recorders
came towards you like locusts,
behind the noise,
ahead of the silence,
midnight's insomnia came
at you with shears;

in the ring all men are stone,
beyond the ropes
men are broken.

MAYA ANGELOU

At last, the year is hotwired to autumn,
a time you feel the season lacking
and nothing is as green as it used to be.
Friends break down like worn cars,
roofs thirst for new shingles,
the spark glint no longer twitches from
wanting eyes, even interviewers come
speckled in grey.

You unhinged all in the laughing curves
of your time. Plays blew up like climbing
weather balloons, your calypso voice sprung
from flaming albums, your pen explained
why the caged mew croons.
Still, mayflies only require one day.
When the world burns the skin you're in,
how long does it take to succeed?

Open it up for our daughters' minds Maya,
let morning's pulse speak with mounted echoes.
When you hate your midnight shade,
long for plumb flaxen hair, battle constructed
images massed against you, how long does
it take to reassemble pieces? How long
does it take to become whole?

NEIL DE GRASSE TYSON

Sometimes, I think this never
happened. That I'm back wrestling
in my Bronx high school,
only I'm the age I am now.
Somewhere, I know, we're
all living parallel lives.

Everything that could happen
is happening right now.
In one universe I'm you
and you're me. In another,
we're not even particles or string,
and Hitler rules this blue orb
from Reichstag windows.

I shadow the observatory's roof.
The constellations are many.
To think, we always look back
in time, to when we invented wheels,
when we were single cells spreading
through Cambrian seas, when we were
stardust lighting life's potential.

I'm watching night skies
coalesce around thoughts,
surprised to still hear
the bare-faced brown
boy's wonder within.

OBAMA

In one life version,
he is floating on Hebrew
cloth set among reeds. A court
woman washes the invincible Nile
from his unscrubbed skin. Surrounded
by etched stone, he grows to shell
palaces with sunlit words.
His voice a cleansing of space.

In another, India asks where
he has been. His incarnation
shores him under the law's shaded
wings. He refuses to swing at England's
red face. Even friends disagree
with the kind largesse of smiles
he presents to enemies.

Still, the world expects miracles.
He is from Hawaii and parts unsung.
Someone said his unearthing failed
geography. No one could possibly
be from where they claim. America's
dehumanizing shadow blows behind him.
He is morning milk and coal hillside.
Like freed slaves scooting north,
he is a man in parts. An enigma fused
in dust. Boy, I mean Mr. President,
show me your birth certificate.

OPRAH WINFREY

It's sweeps season and
hopeful hands rise from the
audience. The day's recording tape
says I will always be here.
The bantam girl who escaped
her past speaks with wave-crashing
confidence, standing one hundred
feet above Times Square.

When I run forward on morning's
treadmill, the future never seems
impossible, even when it appears
in the words of others. When I
back-pedal with clear mind,
the winged present unfolds as it
should. To think the little coal girl
wades thoughts in two billion green
seas. There's nothing left to tell. A
secret has never been more unearthed.
I had a dream, and I shook it!

NOTES

Adoption – Apparently, black dogs and cats are the least adopted.

bell hooks – American intellectual, author, socialist, and feminist.

Benedita da Silva – first female and Afro-Brazilian governor of the state of Rio de Janeiro.

Bill Withers – American singer, songwriter, and musician. Words in italics from "Leavin' on Your Mind" written by Wayne P. Walker and Webb Pierce.

Black Uhuru – Reggae band popular during the 1980's.

Bob Marley – Legendary reggae superstar. *Congo bongo I* taken from the song "Natty Dread".

Bromley Armstrong – Canadian Civil Rights leader. Conducted restaurant sit-ins.

Carlinhos Brown – Brazilian songwriter, musician, and producer. Created Pracatum Project to improve living conditions in his home town.

Carolina Maria de Jesus – Brazilian peasant who spent most of her life in the favelas (slums). Her diary, *Child of the Dark*, became a bestseller, but she died penniless.

Celia Cruz – Revered black salsa singer born in Cuba. Known as the *Queen of Salsa.*

Central Park Five – Five black teenagers who were wrongfully convicted of the brutal rape and homicide of a Central Park jogger.

Coloured Hockey League – All-black Maritimes hockey league 1895–1930.

Convict leasing – A system of penal labour practiced in southern states from 1865–1942. Southern legislatures passed "black codes" to restrict the free movement of blacks and force them into unpaid employment. Armies of young black men, who were guilty of no crimes, were entrapped by ridiculous laws, convicted, and then leased out to plantations and other employers.

Many were entrapped especially during fall harvests. Convict leasing was very lucrative for southern states.

Delos Davis – Second black lawyer in Canada.

Dr. Anderson Abbott – First black Canadian to become a licensed physician.

Elijah McCoy – Black Canadian-American inventor and engineer. Invented efficient ways to lubricate steam engines.

Fela Kuti – Nigerian musician, singer, political activist, and pioneer of Afrobeat. He died from AIDS.

Fred Hampton – Black Panther leader gunned down by police while sleeping in his bed.

George E. Carter – First Canadian-born black Judge.

George Junius Stinney Jr. – At age fourteen, youngest person executed in the USA during the twentieth century. He had no legal representation and his family had to flee town.

Gil Scott-Heron – American soul and jazz poet, musician, and author. Wrote the songs "The Klan" and "Winter in America." Wrote the poem "The Revolution Will Not Be Televised."

Gordon Parks – American photographer, musician, writer, and film director. *The Learning Tree* is one of his films.

Grant Fuhr – All-star NHL goalie. First black player inducted into the Hockey Hall of Fame.

Harry Jerome – Canadian sprinter.

Herb Carneghie – Played professional hockey 1944–54, but was never drafted into NHL due to racism. Founder of the Future Aces Foundation.

Howlin' Wolf – Great blues legend. "Smokestack Lightning" is one of his signature songs.

Ismael Rivera (aka Maelo) – Puerto Rican singer and composer who was very proud of his African heritage.

Jack Johnson – Boxer, first African-American heavyweight champion.

Jarome Iginla – All-star NHL hockey player.

Joe Arroyo – Columbian singer, composer, and musician.

Joe Frazier – Boxer.

John Lee Hooker – Great blues legend. "Serves You Right To Suffer" is one of his signature songs.

John Ware – Former slave turned cowboy who was the first person to bring cattle into Alberta which eventually spawned the ranching industry.

Jorge Ben Jor – Brazilian composer, singer, and musician. Brilliant songwriter who wrote many iconic Brazilian songs including "Mas Que Nada."

Lincoln Alexander – First black MP in House of Commons. First black federal cabinet minister. First black Lieutenant Governor serving Ontario.

Lord Kitchener – Trinidadian calypsonian.

Marie-Joseph Angelique – Slave in New France (Quebec) falsely accused of setting a fire that burned much of Old Montreal. She was executed.

Mary Ann Shadd – First black female publisher in North America and first female publisher in Canada.

Mathieu da Costa – First black person known to have visited Canada.

Miles Davis – Legendary American Jazz musician, trumpet player, composer, and band leader who changed the course of musical history. "'Round Midnight" is a jazz standard by Thelonius Monk.

Mestre Bimba – Legendary master practioner of Afro-Brazilian martial art capoeira. The berimbau is the main capoeira instrument.

Michaëlle Jean – Canada's first Governor General of Caribbean origin.

Neil de Grasse Tyson – American astronomer.

No. 2 Construction Battalion – Only predominantly black battalion in Canadian history. Served in World War I.

Oscar Peterson – Canadian jazz pianist and composer. Won eight Grammy awards.

P.K. Subban – Star defenseman for the Montreal Canadians hockey team.

Paul Robeson – American singer and actor who joined the civil rights movement.

Pit-House – A building partly dug into the ground and covered by a roof. Black Loyalists built these to survive the first few winters in the Maritimes.

Roaring Lion – Legendary Trinidadian calypsonian. The "tamboo bamboo" is a percussive instrument made from bamboo. It's the precursor to the steel pan.

Rose Fortune – A black Loyalist who became a successful business woman and the first female police officer in Canada.

Ruby Bridges – First black child to attend an all-white elementary school.

Sandra de Sá – Brazilian composer and singer known for racially conscious lyrics including the famous "Olhos Coloridos (Coloured Eyes)."

Sparrow – Trinidadian calypsonian originally born in Grenada.

Toussaint Louverture – Leader of the Haitian revolution.

Without Royalties – *Negro streets at dawn* taken from Allen Ginsburg's poem "Howl."

ACKNOWLEDGEMENTS

I exuberantly praise Jim Nason, Heather Woods, Deanna Janovski, and all the diligent and meticulous people at Tightrope Books for accepting and publishing this book!

I tremendously applaud the brilliant and inimitable George Elliott Clarke for his magnificent foreword.

I'm overly grateful to Ruth Roach Pierson for her sagacious and assiduous editing.

Infinite thanks to Krystyna Wesolowska for her superb photography, friendship, and vision.

Thank you to Kalkidan Assefa for the incredible cover art.

Many of the poems were first workshopped by the Plasticine Poets. The Plasticine Poets were: David Clink, James Deahl, Kate Marshall Flaherty, Lisa Richter, Lisa Young, Mary Rykov, Nashira Dernesch, Phoebe Tsang, Robin Richardson, Rod Weatherbie, and Susie Berg. Thanks to Austin Clarke for the idea. Praise to Dorothy Donley, Karri Hutchinson, Fauzya Alarakhiya, Pablo Garcia, and Patrizia Ditillio. I'd like to acknowledge the Canada Council for the Arts, the Ontario Arts Council, and the Toronto Arts Council for their generosity during the writing of this book.

ABOUT THE AUTHOR

Michael Fraser is a Toronto high school teacher, poet, and writer. He has been published in various national and international journals and anthologies, including *The Best Canadian Poetry in English, 2013*. His manuscript, *The Serenity of Stone*, won the 2007 Canadian Aid Literary Award Contest and was published in 2008 by Bookland Press. He won *FreeFall's* 2014 Poetry Contest and is the creator and former director of the Plasticine Poetry Series.

3450